"Dennis has written a practical approach to an issue that plagues so many organizations. Strategic alignment is important for any corporation but it is an absolute imperative for a non-profit organization. There is such a temptation to "follow the money". Additionally, there are so many needs in the world that can easily distract good-hearted people and cause organizations to splinter in various directions."

Thank you Dennis for addressing such a critical challenge to the nonprofit sector!

David Williams, President and Chief Executive Officer
Make-A-Wish' America

"Any organization's impact depends on strong leaders and not just the CEO. Strategic Alignment helps senior leaders harness the power of your non-profits' strategy to achieve even more for those you serve."

Carolyn S. Miles, President & Chief Executive Officer
Save the Children

"This is a must-read book for nonprofit CEOs and board members that highlight the importance of communication and developing an organization's leaders, strategies and goals to be successful. The book really illustrates the key elements to make things happen and getting positive results."

Jonathan R. Pearson, Executive Director, Corporate Philanthropy and Community Affairs
Horizon Blue Cross Blue Shield of New Jersey

"As always Dennis has a no nonsense approach to board development that gets the job done. He has the uncanny ability to move board and staff in the direction they need to go to achieve their desired results. Dennis's methods will challenge, build and align the stakeholders in your organization to achieve success. Another winner from Dennis."

Nancy J. Tringali, CEO
Community Health Charities of the Northeast

"A concise and straightforward read that will help management and board truly achieve success! A must read for the nonprofit board and senior staff to move beyond the strategic planning session and create real momentum and impetus to move their organization to reach its goals and engage a broader constituency. You have helped us use Strategic Alignment to remember why our organization was formed and what we need to do to realize our goals: reengage, revitalize and realign!"

Jeri Schaefer, Executive Director
Princeton Internships in Civic Service
Princeton University

"Drawing on his rich experience as the CEO of several major healthcare organizations and now as a highly regarded consultant to nonprofit organizations, Dennis Miller provides the reader with a succinct yet comprehensive formula for nonprofit organization leaders and boards to maximize their effectiveness and success. He stresses how an organization, in order to have a successful strategic plan, must have a clear and compelling vision; have completed a comprehensive assessment of key strengths and critical weaknesses; possess a comprehensive funding plan; and complete a detailed plan for implementation and execution. I urge senior executives and board leaders of nonprofit organizations to read this book and consider providing it to their senior staff and board members. It should serve as an excellent tool to increase effective communication, strategic planning and maximize organization success."

Charles M. Dombeck, Chairman
National Institute for People with Disabilities in New Jersey

THE POWER OF
STRATEGIC
ALIGNMENT

A Guide to Energizing Leadership
and Maximizing Potential in Today's
Nonprofit Organizations

DENNIS C. MILLER

authorHOUSE®

AuthorHouse™ LLC
1663 Liberty Drive
Bloomington, IN 47403
www.authorhouse.com
Phone: 1-800-839-8640

Published by AuthorHouse 11/05/2013

ISBN: 978-1-4918-2579-2 (sc)
ISBN: 978-1-4918-2639-3 (e)

Library of Congress Control Number: 2013919987

This book is dedicated to the millions and millions of individuals and organizations all around the world who wake up every day dedicated to making a difference in the lives of others.

Contents

ACKNOWLEDGEMENTS

I need to begin by thanking my wonderful editor, Wendy Dodge, whose knowledge of the English language make me look good. She is absolutely the best. Wendy allows me the time to create and focus on content. I feel a great sense of relief every time I receive an email from Wendy for keeping my grammar correct and when something doesn't make sense, she always makes the right suggestion. I owe her a great deal of gratitude which will be difficult to repay. Thank you so much again, Wendy.

I want to thank the many people who helped me with this book including Xiomara Guevara, John McIlquham, Robert Parker, David Flood, Damyn Kelly, Richard Kafaf, Sally Glick, Michael Tozzoli and Jeri Schaefer.

I would also like to thank John Hynes, Andrea Korn-Hauschild, Ellen Brescia and the great team at Korn Hynes Communications for their expert advice and design on the front cover of the book.

Finally, I want to thank my wonderful wife and life partner, Gladys, who always provides the right comments, criticisms and suggestions. Thank goodness I married up.

INTRODUCTION

I have been very fortunate to work with many great people and organizations over the past thirty plus years in the nonprofit sector. All of the executive directors, board members, corporate and foundation officers, volunteers, donors and professional colleagues that I have worked with have had a very positive impact on me. I guess you can say that I have been truly blessed to be associated with such great people. What impresses me the most is their passion and commitment to make a difference in the lives of others. They truly care about others and work tremendously long hours to generate a positive social impact in their communities, often with little financial reward. Their commitment to their respective mission and determination to succeed despite the ever increasing challenges and obstacles inspires me. They are truly some of the most wonderful people I know.

What concerns me the most, however, is how many of them continue to spend an inordinate amount of time and energy without the results and successes they hoped to achieve for their respective organization. Regardless of their purposeful missions and great causes, many struggle to fully engage their boards and stakeholders and develop the resources to survive, let alone succeed or excel. I believe strongly that there is a new smarter way to achieve success in the nonprofit sector.

In my first book, *A Guide to Achieving New Heights: The Four Pillars of Successful Nonprofit Leadership*, my goal was to provide an inspirational and educational book on how to unlock the leadership potential of chief executives, board members and those who aspire to leadership positions in the nonprofit sector. In my second book, *The Nonprofit Board Therapist: A Guide to Unlocking Your Organization's True Potential*, my goal was to provide a road map on how to effectively integrate effective board governance, inspiring leadership, powerful visionary thinking and philanthropic success.

In *The Power of* Strategic *Alignment: A Guide to Energizing Leadership and Maximizing Potential In Today's Nonprofit Organizations*, I will identify the key steps necessary to go beyond the traditional strategic planning process to achieve long term success and sustainability. This innovative concept is called *Strategic Alignment* which refers to the process of aligning all stakeholders, both internally and externally, to be focused and committed to achieving one goal: the organization's vision. In addition, the concept requires the development of new competencies and non-traditional skill sets for both executive and board leadership.

The traditional way most nonprofit organizations embark on their strategic planning process often begins with high hopes, but concludes in disappointment with little achieved and the report often ending up sitting on some executive's shelf collecting dust. This disappointment is commonly the result of most strategic plans lacking the following four components:

- An upfront, comprehensive assessment of the organization to identify key strengths and crucial areas of needed improvement;
- A clear vision with established measures of successful progress to align the entire organization's efforts;
- A comprehensive funding plan to secure the necessary resources, and;
- A detailed plan for implementation and execution with buy-in from both the board and staff.

For nearly a decade, I have performed numerous organizational and/or board performance assessment studies. What became very obvious to me when conducting these assessments was the absolute lack of any real alignment of the organization in pursuit of an agreed upon vision. Many times the organization did not have a vision or future direction to follow. Even those who indicated they had a vision statement admitted it was often not more than a meaningless statement about "becoming all things to all people" or something like that. There was no organized plan of action to incorporate the work of the board and the efforts of the leadership team and staff towards this vision. Everyone worked very hard on many strategic initiatives but they were not all aligned towards a common goal. Nor was their culture of performance aligned towards the effort of collaboration and respect. To my amazement, far too many leadership teams never even take the time to collectively discuss the many strategic issues facing their own organization. Never. They are all too busy. No wonder they struggle to survive, let alone succeed!

It became apparent to me that to successfully assist an organization in truly developing a strategic plan, all of their goals and actions necessary to achieve a vision have to be fully aligned. The entire organization, including the work of the board, leadership and staff has to be restructured to require individual goals to be fully aligned with organizational goals. Everyone has to be on the same page and motivated towards the one compelling goal—achieving the organization's vision. In essence, the organization needs to be in *Strategic Alignment*. Too many organizations focus solely on the external environmental challenges during the strategic planning when the major reason most organizations fail is their inability to address their internal obstacles. The overwhelming reason most nonprofit organizations fail is the result of not adequately addressing their internal issues and not because of their response to the changing environmental landscape of the sector. Internal obstacles often include the lack of trust and respect among senior managers, stale programs, board members who have stayed far too long and the lack of contemporary leadership skill sets. An organization needs to honestly address both challenges, internal and external, in order to be in *Strategic Alignment*.

The "silo mentality" that so many organizations were working under is no longer acceptable and actually extremely detrimental to their very survival. Far worse, too many organizations have unresolved internal issues and conflicts preventing them from working more effectively together. The idea of a senior management team not talking, respecting or trusting each other has to be dealt with "head on" and eliminated. The culture of "my needs first" has to be transformed to "those we serve first." There are enough external obstacles that every organization has to face but to also have to deal constantly with their internal obstacles of personality and egos is wasting valuable energy and time. A new effort to fully align the entire organization has to be developed. I begin to facilitate my strategic planning clients by first performing an organizational wide assessment to determine their strategic alignment or lack thereof towards their vision. Everything began to make more sense when I realized they needed a "coach and facilitator" to help with the implementation of their strategic alignment.

Recently, I asked a number of clients who completed their strategic planning process with me under my new "strategic alignment approach" to describe "What has the process done for you?" The typical responses that I expected were "It provided us with a clear path forward" or "helped transform the organization" or "really engaged our board." I have heard these responses before and I was always very pleased to hear them express their satisfaction with my work. However, I began to hear from many of my clients that "you helped revitalize our organization". They told me that they now felt a greater sense of confidence to achieve their strategic goals and the know-how to accomplish them. They indicated that my new process of *Strategic Alignment* reenergized the entire board and staff and they were excited "to know who they were and where they were going."

I will also describe the new competencies and skill sets required of today's nonprofit leaders as well as the characteristics of high performing nonprofit boards. Today, more than ever before, the chief executive and board must be true partners in leading the organization forward to generate the positive social impact needed in their communities. In order for your organization to successfully pursue its vision and goals, it must be in *Strategic Alignment*. Organizations that are in *Strategic Alignment* have these characteristics:

- Strong organizational self-knowledge
- Engaged key stakeholders
- Inspiring vision
- Entrepreneurial Leaders
- High performing boards
- Impactful programs and services
- Achievement and outcome driven
- Investors seeking to contribute
- Commitment to continuous improvement
- Recognized for excellence

As you read this book, you will learn on how to dramatically increase your organizational alignment and began to achieve new and dramatic levels of success. You will come away from reading this book with:

1. A new way to embark on a more effective strategic planning process to build organizational capacity for long term sustainability;
2. The hope, courage and motivation to achieve dramatically better results for your organization;
3. A greater sense of purpose and self-confidence to empower you to feel more hopeful and passionate and less stressful about what you need to do:
4. Being able to approach your work with a higher level of energy and a positive attitude knowing the best practices of others and how to implement them.

5. Knowing how to truly revitalize and "impart new life to your organization" through *Strategic Alignment*.

There may be a particular chapter in *Strategic Alignment* that you may want to read first, but you should read this book in its entirety. In this way, you will gain a much better understanding of how to successfully initiate and complete the strategic planning process. This book will include the following chapters:

- The Assessment—How to Discover Your Organization's Soul
- The Vision—What Are Your Dreams
- The Process—How to Build Your Plan
- Executive Leadership: Why Today's CEO Means Chief Entrepreneurial Officer
- High Performing Boards—How to Fully Engage Your Board
- Impactful Programs and Services—When to Collaborate, Affiliate or Merge
- The Positive Brand—What Do People Know Us For
- Seeking Investors, Not Just Funders—Why Giving to Success Makes $ense
- Successfully Executing The Plan—How to Build the Bicycle While Riding It

I hope you enjoy this book and come away revitalized. Let's now turn our attention to Step One—The Assessment—How to Discover Your Organizational Soul.

THE ASSESSMENT

How to Discover Your Organizational Soul

"Your visions will become clear only when you can look into your own heart. Who looks outside, dreams; who looks inside, awakes."
—C.G. Jung

Very few of us can imagine having a physician perform surgery without first having thoroughly examined the patient. The ordering of X-rays, blood work and conducting a complete medical examination are standard procedure before performing surgery. No one can imagine a surgeon making an incision of the body and *THEN* asking why am I performing surgery on this patient? Only by carefully listening to the patient's complaints and symptoms and reviewing the results of all medical tests can a physician determine a future course of treatment based on a sound diagnosis.

Yet so often we embark upon a strategic planning process without first performing a comprehensive assessment of them. Traditionally, the most common approach to performing such an assessment is the SWOT analysis (strengths, weaknesses, opportunities and threats). Based on my experience, however, most SWOT analyses are rarely effective in assisting an organization in getting to know their "organizational soul"—who are they and where are they really at?

Before all of my SWOT critics scream too loudly, I completely agree that knowing your strengths is the crucially important first step towards building your organizational capacity for success. I also agree that it is crucial to assist an organization in identifying their areas of needed improvement. But my difference in approach goes way beyond just the terms "weaknesses" and "areas of improvement." Areas of improvement need to be based on a comprehensive knowledge of best practices that an organization will need to develop to achieve their vision and dreams (more on this in later chapters). These areas need to include board governance, leadership development, program and service capacity, strategic planning, marketing & public relations and fundraising & development. Far too often the SWOT analysis identifies areas of "weakness" that are too limited in scope and fail to provide the know-how to convert these areas into strengths.

Even questions about "opportunities and threats" are stated without first spending the time to fully get to know the client's vision for the future. There will always be opportunities and threats but far too often SWOT comes up too short in assisting the organization build the necessary organizational capacity to achieve their vision. The one question many often ask after a SWOT analysis is conducted is *"So tell me exactly how this information is going to help me?"* I have seen far too many clients who previously had a SWOT analysis performed who still have no clue as how to improve and build a stronger organizational capacity for success.

In order to conduct a comprehensive organizational assessment, confidential interviews with key members of the Board, executive team and other key stakeholders need to be scheduled. Prior to conducting these interviews, the following information needs to be reviewed:

- Board minutes for the past twelve months
- Prior strategic plan, if any
- Notes from prior retreats, if any
- Management table of organization
- Board member names and professional backgrounds
- Board structure and committees
- Most recent financial audit
- List of all programs and services with statistics for past three years
- Marketing and public relations communications and reports including any recent Annual Reports
- Fundraising results for the past three years

These interviews can be scheduled either at the organization's site, board member office or other convenient place and take approximately sixty minutes each, except the CEO and Board Chair are normally scheduled for ninety minutes each. The interviews should be conducted in a quiet setting where uninterrupted conversation can take place. Restaurants (or other loud place like a sporting event) should be avoided at all times unless this is the only time and place that an important stakeholder is available. For those that cannot schedule a face-to-face interview, a limited number of telephone conference calls should be permitted. When conducting assessments for nationally based organizations, they often require that all interviews be conducted via conference call on Skype due to geographic locations of the board members. These interviews are often very productive as well, but face-to-face is preferred.

It goes without saying that only an experienced objective facilitator with extensive knowledge of nonprofit organizations should be engaged to perform the assessment. All who have either a biased, prejudiced or previously determined opinion need not apply. Having someone from within the organization is a recipe for disaster and I would highly discourage this option.

The questions asked should be open ended to enable the interviewee the opportunity to answer fully based on his or her own perspective. Many times during the interview process, an interviewee tells me that he or she can only answer the question based on his or her own perspective. I inform them that only his or her perspective is all I am interested in hearing about. Open ended questions begin with words such as how, when, what or who. Occasionally I ask a question and ask for a response between one and ten, for example, "On a scale of one to ten, with ten being the highest, how would you rate the effectiveness of the board of trustees?"

Objectives of the assessment process include determining answers to the following:

- Is there a clearly articulated vision?
- Is the organization strategically aligned to achieve the vision?
- How effective is executive leadership?
- How effective is the board in performing their work?
- How motivated and engaged is the board?

- What obstacles are there to developing governance best practices?
- Are the top achievements effectively communicated to stakeholders?
- How does the board measure success?
- What is the image/brand in the community?
- Is there an annual evaluation of leadership performance?
- Does the board evaluate their own performance?
- What success has been achieved with fundraising?
- Is the organization financially sustainable if current operations continue?
- What are their hopes for the outcome of the process?

People have often asked me why I need to read the board minutes as part of the assessment. The answer is quite simple: By reading the minutes, I can detect trends that either are or are not being resolved, not being addressed, or wondering why there has been no mention of certain expected topics. For example, a foundation client's minutes never reflected a discussion of how much money was being raised. When the board chair was asked about this, he stated that the foundation's role was to invest the money already raised and there was no need to raise additional dollars. When I mentioned his answer to the CEO, he almost had a heart attack. "That's the problem with them, they are not doing their job." Similar to the reason a physician orders x-rays is the reason I request the minutes, they can tell me a lot about the organization early on in the process.

Clearly if the leadership cannot effectively describe their vision, it implies the critical need to assist them in developing one. By probing the effectiveness of executive leadership and/or board governance, you can easily identify areas for improvement and/or obstacles to address. It is critically important during the assessment process to identify leadership and management who are not performing their duties at the required level. The biggest reason nonprofit organizations fail to achieve success is their inability to confront poor performance at all levels. Another crucial area for assessment is how effectively the organization does or does not communicate their key achievements, successes and positive outcomes to their respective community stakeholders. By reviewing the marketing and public relations communications, one can easily determine if they are reporting on "what they do" or "what they have achieved." Far too often, the annual report is filled with statistics on the number and amount of activity that they are involved in, but little communication about their achievements and outcomes. This is especially critical when one realizes that today more people give to "success than distress" and donate towards "making a difference in others" rather than in "helping you address your needs." When we get to the chapters on marketing/branding and fundraising, the need to address and communicate your organization's achievements will become clearly more evident.

The information obtained during the review process and the results of the interviews will be of tremendous significance in determining the following:

- How to best facilitate a consensus towards achieving a vision
- How strategically aligned is the organization today towards achieving its vision

- What are the internal obstacles preventing the organization from being more successful
- What best practices need to be developed
- What will be the organization's priorities for implementation
- How to effectively engage all key stakeholders in the process

The initial draft findings need to be discussed in-depth with the executive officer and board leadership and only then presented and discussed with the entire board. The presentation should begin with all identified organizational strengths and then progress to the areas of needed improvement necessary to strengthen organizational capacity.

Let's now turn our attention to Step Two—The Vision: What Are Your Dreams?

THE VISION

What Are Your Dreams?

*"The only thing worse than being blind
is having sight but no vision."*
—Helen Keller

Sometimes in life the simplest things can be the most difficult. This is often the case with creating your organization's vision. Mostly everyone knows that mission answers the question "What is your purpose?" and that vision answers "Where are you going?" I really don't know why, but just asking the simple question "What is your vision?" can be the biggest strategic challenge most organizations have to confront. Perhaps because we are all mired in our day to day struggles with our long term planning horizon not going beyond next week, most of us have a difficulty answering this question. Often times they answer by citing their purpose or "We just want to survive." Though often a true statement, it will not inspire your key stakeholders to be motivated going forward.

Yet in spite of the challenge, one must answer this question before any effective strategic plan can proceed. This is important because it sets the stage for leadership to chart a new direction or future view of the organization. As a former CEO, I know first-hand of the daily difficulties and challenges everyone faces in managing the day-to-day operations of our organizations. Still, a leader needs to articulate the vision and build a strategic plan to make the vision become a reality. In days gone by, the board set the vision and management was told to implement the plan to achieve it. Today, an effective leader must work in partnership with the board to create the organization's future direction. They don't wait for their boards to create the vision, they have the courage to develop and communicate their hopes for the future. It takes courage to set the vision.

According to Burt Nanus, author of Visionary Leadership and several other books on leadership, vision is a realistic, credible, attractive future for your organization. Your vision is your articulation of a destination towards which your organization should aim, a future that in many important ways is better, more successful, or more desirable than your present. It is a signpost pointing the way for all who need to understand what the organization is and where it intends to go. Nanus goes on to state that "Successful leaders know that nothing drives an organization like an attractive, worthwhile, achievable vision for the future."

Based on my experience, your vision should set standards of excellence, inspire enthusiasm, encourage commitment, and be well articulated and easily understood. Above all, your vision should be ambitious.

Questions:
- What is your organization's vision for the future?
- Has your current vision become stale and in need of revitalization?
- Are you still passionate about achieving it?

- Is your new vision a realistic, credible, attractive future for your organization?
- Will it inspire your staff, board, donors and other stakeholders to be to achieve it?

Want to think "out of the box?" How about adding the following topic of discussion to your agenda at your next board meeting: Let's call the meeting to order. Do I have a motion to approve the minutes? A second? Thanks. Okay, we are going to discuss our vision statement today and determine if it is still inspiring us or in need of revitalization? Talk about shock and awe! These conversations obviously require more time than a regular board meeting can provide, but certainly should be a topic at your next retreat. If you really want to "refresh the thinking of everyone in your organization," plan to address this topic in the near term.

It is crucial for every organization to honestly evaluate their vision statements. I had a college client with a vision statement that was three paragraphs long and prominently displayed throughout the organization. When I asked the president if the statement was inspiring anyone he said no, but too many people in the organization were involved in creating it to change it now. Far too many vision statements are not inspirational, not realistic nor an attractive future for your organization, yet we continue to claim they are. Many of us even struggle to identify someone who is visionary. People who attend my strategic planning workshops are asked to identify individuals who they know or have heard of who are or were visionary. Sounds simple, right? But beyond the famous names of George Washington, Martin Luther King, Charles

Lindberg, Albert Einstein, Steve Jobs and Bill Gates, most of them struggle to identify someone.

Questions:
- Who would you name as being visionary thinkers and leaders?
- What do you think is required to be a visionary leader?
- Do you have the drive and persistence to achieve your vision?

There are actually thousands and thousands of individuals living in every city and state in our country who are providing inspirational leadership in their communities. Every day I learn of another individual who is inspiring others to improve their communities and those who live there. Whether it deals with social justice, early childhood education, drug addiction, social science, environment, arts & culture or a myriad of other great causes, visionary leadership is providing important changes all around us.

What is common about visionary thinkers is their passion, courage, confidence and strength of will. Leaders who are visionary are willing to take calculated risks and possess the attribute of persistence. Unabashed persistence allows the visionary leader to confront and overcome all of the difficulties they face, including the opposition of others, insufficient resources and bad fortune. The major difference between a successful visionary person and an unsuccessful one often comes down to drive and persistence. Visionary leaders also possess an unusually large degree of openness to new ideas and information. Inflexible people usually cannot be persuaded to search for new information, once they make up their minds, nothing will move them. Those who provide visionary leadership are open to experimentation and going beyond the status quo.

Okay, so now you know the definition of a vision and have a better understanding of the leadership skills necessary to achieve it, but how do you actually create the vision? The following are a few suggestions:

1. Develop a steering committee of creative and future thinking stakeholders. This group usually consists of key stakeholders who know your organization well (key employees, management team and/or board members). Ask each member of the committee to describe in general terms what their vision is for the organization. Sometimes their vision is about the kind of community they want to create or what your organization look like in the future. Write each vision on a flip chart and ask the group the following questions for each statement:

    *   Is this a more attractive future than the present?
    *   Is it realistic and credible?
    *   Will it generate passion, excitement and commitment to achieve?
    *   Does it further your mission?

If the answer is yes to each question, congratulations, you have your vision. If the answers are more no than yes, get back to work.

2. Schedule a board or leadership retreat to repeat the above in small group settings and facilitate the results of each group discussion. Also, ask each group to discuss among themselves the critical issues facing the organization. List these issues in order of fundamental importance. Then discuss ways to resolve or address each issue. The future direction for your organization may become much clearer after these discussions.

3. Instead of focusing your attention on the critical issues as above, discuss the major goals that each would like your organization to achieve. After lengthy discussion and agreement upon your goals, a future picture of your organization will probably develop.

4. Go on a hike in a pleasant environment or sit on a comfortable chair without any distractions and dream about the future of your organization. Do not allow your day-to-day challenges and obstacles to limit your horizons. Dream about the ideal situation and consider that dream your organization's vision.

Creating a vision can be a highly motivating process to inspire everyone to produce the desired outcomes: achieving your vision and realizing your organization's full potential. For those of you who remember playing the game of Monopoly (don't pass go and don't collect $200), do not proceed to develop a strategic plan without first successfully creating your vision. If there is no dream to achieve, what are you building a plan for anyway?

Now that you have created your vision, strategic goals and a plan to achieve them have to be developed. Strategic goals are statements of what you need to achieve in order for your vision to become a reality. They should reflect the analysis performed in your assessment which identified your strengths and key areas needing improvement.

Let's turn now to Step Three—The Process: How to Build Your Plan.

THE PROCESS

How to Build Your Plan

"Intellectual strategies alone will not motivate
people. Only an organization with a real mission
or sense of purpose that comes out of an intuitive
or spiritual dimension will capture people's hearts.
And you must have people's hearts to inspire the
hard work required to realize a vision."
—John Naisbett and Patricia Aburdene,
Reinventing the Corporation

Now that you're ready to develop your strategic plan, let's
address a few basic issues:

Questions:
- How will you achieve your vision?
- What are the right strategies to accomplish it?
- What specific actions are needed to be taken and
  by whom?

The following are ten major points on developing your
plan:

1. Engage as many of your key stakeholders as
   possible. You will find that people are more

committed to your plan when they were asked to participate in its development.

2. Stay focused on the crucial issues identified in your assessment. I have seen too much time and energy wasted by spending an inordinate amount of time on issues and information that are not critical to creating your organization's future success.

3. Keep the process simple. Don't make it any more complex than necessary.

4. Make sure you seek good ideas from everyone. Listen to your stakeholders different points of view. Encourage people to speak candidly about their hopes for the organization and what they would like to see accomplished. It is amazing to learn how many organizations never consider asking their key donors to participate in their strategic planning process, yet get disappointed when they don't contribute to their expected potential.

5. Build a plan that is connected to people's heartfelt emotions. If people are not passionate about the plan, they will most likely not participate in its implementation at the level required for success.

6. Invest the required time to develop an implementation plan. The biggest reason for failure is not properly investing the time and resources for execution. Though we will address this later in the book, it is critical to ask the following questions:

- Who will be responsible for what specific action?

- What is the timeline for completion?
- What will be the process for communicating plan updates?
- Does everyone know what is expected of them?

7. Focus on results and deal decisively with all obstacles your organization faces in producing the desired outcomes. While the perceived obstacle to success is external, the reality is that more organizations fail because they cannot resolve their internal conflicts.

8. Be prepared to modify your implementation plan based on new information that becomes available.

9. Communicate your plan to all key stakeholders. It is amazing how many people have told me "They asked for my input, but then never got back to me on the final results of the plan." It is more and more important today to promote your achievements and successful results. If you don't tell them, who will?

10. Make sure you have developed a list of success factors for measuring and monitoring your progress. Creating a one-page Scorecard for your Board members and leadership team is a great way for everyone to focus on the important issues. Place a green dot on those strategies where progress is being achieved, a yellow dot where the outcome is less certain but still a work in progress and a red dot when nothing is being achieved at the current time. In order to spend your time wisely, focus on red dots first and then yellow dots second. Spending all of your time patting

yourselves on the back for those green dots may leave the others unaddressed and results hard to come by.

I always advise my clients to focus on a few important goals. Whenever an organization tells me they are working on ten different goals, I always know that their chance of actually achieving anything goes down dramatically. Have you ever really achieved anything when you have more than four goals at a time? For most of you, the honest answer is no. Another bit of good advice is to make sure that your goals have the following characteristics:

1. Specific—they must be clear and easily understood.
2. Measurable—if you cannot measure your goals, how will you know if you are ever really achieving them?
3. Attainable—they must be realistic, yet a bit of a stretch to achieve.
4. Relevant—they must be an important tool in reaching your organization's vision
5. Timetables—they must have beginnings and ending points.

Let's now turn to Step Four—Executive Leadership: Why Every CEO Needs to be the Chief Entrepreneurial Officer.

EXECUTIVE LEADERSHIP

Why Today's CEO Means Chief Entrepreneurial Officer

"Management is doing things right;
leadership is doing the right things"
—*Peter F. Drucker*

As a board member, what leadership skills would you seek to recruit for if your executive director announced that he or she were resigning or retiring from his or her position?

Questions:
- Would you seek to replace your current executive director's leadership skills with similar skill sets?
- Would you identify a whole new set of required leadership skills before you did your search?
- Has your board discussed the issue of succession planning?
- Does your board have a good understanding of the leadership skills required to succeed in today's challenging times?

Be prepared to answer this question. Recent studies have shown that over 50% of current executive directors expect to move on from their positions in the next five to seven years. Traditionally, skill sets ranging from having a passion for the mission, program development, securing grants, community relations and overall good management skills were sought when hiring an executive director.

Today, the executive leadership skills required for an organization to succeed have changed dramatically. In this chapter, we will address the new leadership requirements that will be needed to navigate and lead your organization towards achievement of your vision. The following are today's required competencies:

- Visionary thinker
- Entrepreneur
- Relationship builder
- Achievement driven
- Collaborator
- Inspirational motivator

Leaders need to be visionary thinkers. As we discussed in the chapter on Vision, today's executive directors need to chart the future direction for their organizations and communicate it to all stakeholders. Being a visionary thinker is reflective of the entire new competencies required for today's nonprofit leaders. Whereas in the past the board may have set the vision, more and more board members are asking executives to step forward and demonstrate their leadership by stating their vision. Though it is crucial to collaborate and initiate discussions with your board on the topic, you must take the first step. It requires courage to set the vision but others will be inspired and motivated by your inspiration to chart a new course. William Bennis, an American scholar, consultant and author, who is widely regarded as a pioneer in the contemporary field of leadership studies, states "Great things are accomplished by talented people who believe they will accomplish them." I couldn't have said it better!

Having an entrepreneurial spirit is perhaps the most significant competency required by today's nonprofit leaders. Executive Directors need to become the Chief Entrepreneurial Officer (CEO) for their organization. Whereas in the past executives had to manage their organization's revenue, today they need to creatively build the revenue base by generating investments for the organization. It's a whole new ball game! They need to create revenue by building relationships with those willing to invest in them. In the for-profit world, chief executives are paid for increasing their stock price and improving the net worth of their investors. The nonprofit leaders of today need to do something very similar.

In my first book, *A Guide to Achieving New Heights: The Four Pillars of Successful Nonprofit Leadership*, I described having a nonprofit stock price. This "stock price" was increased by positive achievements of your organization, effective communication newsletters and reports, board members who serve as ambassadors promoting your good will, friend and fund development initiatives and creating an overall positive winning attitude among all stakeholders. The higher your stock price, the greater the likelihood that people will want to invest in your success. Leaders should also be rewarded for increasing their stock price and generating significant investments. Maybe you can add this to your next Personnel Committee agenda!

Another competency that a leader must have is the ability to build trusting relationships. This is one area where you cannot hire or delegate someone to do something on your behalf. Organizations whose leaders are able to bring out the best in others, whose leaders are able to make people feel important, whose leaders make people feel that their voices, concerns and actions do matter are the organizations that will be the most successful. For all the nonprofit executive directors who "think they can do it alone" without the support of their employees, think again. As an old saying goes (one of my favorites) "People may not remember what you did, they may not remember what you said, but they will always remember how you made them feel." I learned a long time ago that a leader's job is to help your staff understand the importance of their respective roles and that their input is important. Productivity and accomplishments of objectives are based on getting people to realize that their individual goals are tied into achieving organizational goals.

One key part of building relationships is being able to establish your credibility with your colleagues. Whenever you consistently make decisions that benefit the organization, decisions that align with the organization's mission, you will earn people's trust and respect. Please remember that you may have formal authority through your status and title, but people's respect is really gained through your informal authority; people's trust and admiration for you. Leaders win hearts by your passion, vision and sincerity. It's also extremely important for your employees to know that you are "there for them." To foster trust, talk to people at all levels of your organization. Tell your employees and volunteers about your plans for the future and how they participate in its success. Watch your actions, because people will watch how you treat others and how you communicate with them. One final thought on relationship building relates to keeping promises. It is imperative that you keep your promises, however, when you made a commitment that you can no longer keep, own up to it and let them know the reasons why you had to change your mind. They may not like your decision, however, telling them the honest reason why lets them know that you have your integrity. If you make a promise to do something, deliver on it, if you cannot own up to it with honesty and truthfulness.

Another new core competency for today's nonprofit leaders is being the Chief Branding Officer (CBO). Though we will discuss the concept of building a positive brand identity for your organization in a later chapter, it is important to discuss being a CBO. The chief executive is the face of the organization. Though sometimes the board chair takes on this role, it is more and more the need of the executive director to be the chief communicator proudly letting everyone know of your achievements and results (thereby increasing your stock price!).

Questions:
- When was the last time as executive director or as a board member that you discussed your recent achievements
- How do you communicate to your staff and board about your achievements?
- How does the community that you serve know about your successes?
- How do your donors and prospective donors know about your achievements?

Nonprofit organizations traditionally informed their stakeholders on the number of programs and services they offered, how many people they served, how many tickets they sold and other organizational statistics. These facts were often thought of as indicators of organizational success. The reality today is that funders or investors are more interested in your achievements, outcomes and positive results. They want a return on their investment. Today's nonprofit leaders need to build your organization's positive brand through constant communication of your achievements and success. Don't be afraid to toot your own horn. Organizations that effectively communicate their successes are often highly successful in fundraising. This is not a coincidence.

We discussed the concept of collaboration earlier in the book when we discussed building programs and services. It is important to discuss it again from an executive leadership point of view. Far too often, executives have been concerned with control. The more programs they control the greater their perceived empire. Today, the opposite is true—the more a leadership can initiate discussions around collaboration, their chances of success increase. We live in a time where resources that were once plentiful have now become greatly diminished. In recruiting and rewarding existing leaders, seek those whose personality allows them to be more collaborative and less controlling. Reward and encourage collaboration at all times.

In an article entitled *Towards a New Kind of Collaboration—A Networked Approach to Social Change* by Venture Philanthropy Partners in Washington, D.C., they state that "it seems that almost everywhere you go these day's funders are talking about ways to foster and increase collaboration." However, today when funders talk about collaborating, nonprofits often hear the term as a code for merger. To consider teaming up with a competitor requires a whole new way of leadership thinking and behavior. It requires trust which is often hard to come by these days. Too many "silo mentalities" in the sector need to be broken down that a competitive funding environment creates. We need to begin to think differently. We need to step back and think through the many potential benefits of collaboration—areas where time and effort put into coordinating with others strategically could result in greater returns for the organizations and those they serve. In another article called *The Networked Nonprofit* by Jane Wei-Skillern and Sonia Marciano in a Stanford Social Innovation Review article, they state "By mobilizing resources outside their immediate control, nonprofits can achieve their mission far more efficiently, effectively and sustainably than they could have done by working alone."

Today's nonprofit leaders also need to be inspirational motivators to their staff, boards, donors and other key stakeholders. When resources are few and many employees are going without any pay increase for years, they will still perform their work at a very high level when they are led by inspiring leaders. Why are some organizations successful and others are not? The answer lies in the passion of their leaders; their unending search for excellence in all they do. They listen and actively seek input from their employees and board members. They earn people's respect and trust, they don't demand it. As leaders, they constantly reexamine their organizations from top to bottom. They set expectations for their staff and board, they communicate those expectations and hold people accountable for measuring up. And more importantly, they create a winning attitude that conveys the message to all that their organization is "the place to be" and share this with their stakeholders.

Last but not least, today's leaders need to have the three C's—courage, confidence and competence. All can be achieved with the qualities of these three traits.

Let's now turn to Step Five—High Performing Boards: How to Fully Engage Your Board.

HIGH PERFORMING BOARDS

How to Fully Engage Your Board

*"Never doubt that a small group of thoughtful,
concerned citizens can change the world.
Indeed it is the only thing that ever has."*
—Margaret Mead

If today's nonprofit leader is the Chief Entrepreneurial Officer, what are the requirements of today's board in order to be in *Strategic Alignment* with the vision and goals of the organization? In the well written book "Governance as Leadership: Reframing the Work of Nonprofit Boards" written by Richard P. Chait, et al., the authors described four stages of board governance:

1. A *Founding* board does almost all of the work of the organization, often without any paid staff. This is the primary role of a board in a new and developing organization.
2. A *Fiduciary* role generally emerges after staff have been hired to carry on the work. Here the board sets goals, policies and the direction for the staff to implement.
3. As an organization matures, the board takes on a more *Strategic* role and works together with the staff to develop and implement the strategic plan.

4. The fourth stage of a board's developing role is one of *Leadership*. Though the fiduciary and strategic roles remain important, providing leadership to the organization "in partnership" with the chief executive is the ideal role for an organization desiring to succeed. In this stage, board governance is accomplished by asking the right questions, putting forth new ideas and challenges, and partnering with the chief executive to continually refresh and renew the organization's goals.

Questions:
- What stage of board governance is your organization functioning at now?
- What role does the CEO and board chair play in engaging your board?
- What are the characteristics today of a high performing board?
- What are the common obstacles to such performance?

Based on my experience, a mature board functions in a true partnership with the chief executive. The board is an active participant and assumes a leadership role in guiding the organization towards its vision. One of the characteristics of a high performing board is the level of engagement between the board and chief executive. There needs to be a constant open dialogue about the key issues the organization is facing and how best to utilize the talents, experience and knowledge of each respective board member. It is the responsibility of both the board chair and chief executive to make sure each board member is engaged and an active participant. One of the major complaints that I hear from board members when I perform a board performance assessment is their lack of engagement with the organization. Each respective board member has talents that need to be "tapped" into. For some, community outreach is their expertise, for another, it might be social media, for another, it might be financial planning, but it is crucial that every board member be actively engaged in the pursuit of your vision and goals.

Today an organization can no longer afford to have what I describe as "the rubber band theory of board members." This occurs when a board member parks their car in the lot, removes the rubber band around the board package, which was sent earlier in the week, and begins to read the material for the first time while walking into the meeting. After raising their hand to "second" a motion or two, they put the rubber band back on their board packet and drive home, only to think about the organization again when next month's meeting is about to take place.

Effective board recruitment and reappointment are also key characteristics of a high performing board. For most boards, recruitment happens when members of the board are asked if they know of anyone who might be interested in serving on the board. There is nothing wrong with this process. However, it usually limits you to only those individuals your board members know, not those who you may need to know. My recommendation is to progress from focusing on nominating to recruitment. To start this process, develop an ideal board matrix. This should consist of the sought after expertise you desire on your board, e.g., marketing and public relations, philanthropy, etc. Next identify are there are any key businesses or corporations with a history of community support that would be ideal to have represented on the board. Then identify if there are any geographical areas that you want to have represented on the board. Sometimes an organization can have too many board members from one town and too few from other key communities. The answers to the above is your ideal board matrix. Now, compare the above information with your current matrix of expertise, corporate and business and geographical board members. The difference between the ideal board matrix and your current matrix becomes your priority area for board recruitment. Through research on newspapers, business journals, chambers of commerce and other potential sources, you may identify individuals and businesses that you wish to recruit for your board. Now work the process of finding out who may know someone to get to another. Today's recruitment process is not just nominating someone you know but in recruiting someone that would be most beneficial to raising the profile of the organization.

The other side of recruitment is board reappointment. Highly performing boards have clearly defined and articulated expectations of their individual board members. It is important to have board approved criteria on which to evaluate the performance on individual members. Prior to being reappointed to another term on the board, the Governance Committee should ask each member to submit a self-evaluation. This evaluation should be compared to the board approved criteria for reappointment, and only after careful discussion and debate, should a vote be taken to either approve or not approve another term for the member. Criteria for reappointment may consist of, but not be limited to, attending a minimum number of board meetings, active participation on board committees, attendance at special events, an annual financial contribution, and good ambassadorship in the community. The most difficult issue to address is not reappointing individuals who are no longer motivated and enthusiastic about helping the organization grow. In my experience, not addressing poor board performance is a major reason for organizational performance.

Questions:
- Does your board have an ideal recruitment matrix?
- What are your recruitment priorities?
- Does your board have written reappointment criteria?
- Has your board ever not reappointed someone based on poor performance?
- How does your board ensure leadership succession?

Board leadership succession planning is another characteristic of a high performing board. I believe that someone should not automatically assume the board chair role because they were a board officer moving up the "chairs." I do think it is very important to identify leadership potential from existing board members and the position should be earned and given to those who deserve it through performance, not just longevity. Succession planning ensures that the organization will have stability at the board chair level which is crucial to achieving success. Far too many organizations go "into crisis" when the board chair announced that they will be stepping down from the board. The time for identifying a board chair "in waiting" is not during a crisis but should begin once a new chair assumes their position. In addition, the issue of board leadership qualities should be identified during the recruitment process. Though not everyone recruited to serve on your board may wish to be considered for the role of chair, it's best to identify their potential early on.

As outlined in "The Board Chair Handbook" written by William and Linda Dietel, the duties of the nonprofit board chair bear little resemblance to the job of a "board chair" in the for-profit world. In the latter, the board chair is also the chief executive officer and thus involved in managing the organization's overall operations. The board chair for a non-profit organization has drastically different responsibilities and focuses more on the big picture, keeping an eye on the institution's mission, vision and long term sustainability. The board chair must be a strong strategic thinker who is able to make difficult decisions and willing to be accountable for the organization's sustainability. While the board chair is the chief volunteer officer and is charged with providing leadership to the board, the entire weight of the board's work does not fall completely on one person's shoulder. The board chair needs to delegate to and empower the board committees to do their work and encourage each member of the board to take ownership of their assigned responsibilities. Therefore, selecting the best person available to become board chair is crucial. Here are eight specific actions that can be undertaken by your current board chair to ensure proper leadership succession:

1. Begin as soon as possible to assess the leadership talent of current board members and identify potential candidates for succession
2. Institute ongoing board training for all board members
3. Offer the chair-elect a professional board coach or mentor
4. Ensure that the work of the current board is done efficiently
5. Find ways to recognize and reward your board members for the job they do
6. Provide opportunities for all board members to participate in a wide array of committees, task forces and advisory boards
7. Highlight the achievement and success of the organization and create the winning attitude as "the place to be." People want to belong to winning organizations.
8. Serve as a positive role model. If you appear to enjoy your position and feel good about yourself, the chances are much greater that someone will be willing to assume the leadership role on the board

Boards that focus on performance results and outcomes engage their members and are also an indication of high performance. I remember once facilitating a board retreat about a decade ago and I asked the board members to describe to me their top two achievements of the previous year. There was dead silence, then someone yelled out that they did their budget on time. I told them no one cared. Finally, a woman in the back of the room stated that a very important program they were doing for children was called PALS—Peace: An Alternative

Learning System. This program helped children who were victims of either domestic or sexual abuse learn how to trust people again and build healthy relationships. Now that was an achievement. I asked them how well they communicated this success to external stakeholders and they said, "Not really well." I indicated that it is crucial today, more than ever before to communicate your achievements and results. If you don't, who will?

Questions:
- How does your board measure performance and outcomes?
- How does your board measure and define your success?
- How effective do you communicate your success to key stakeholders?

Boards that are in *Strategic Alignment* with their organization's vision spend more time in board meetings discussing the future than in discussing the past. Ask yourself this question: Does your board spend more or less than 50% of meeting time talking about future issues. Those that are spending too much time discussing yesterday, need to reevaluate the work of their committees or management performance. The more the board creates a culture of success with emphasis on results and achievements, the more the organization will internalize these expectations rise to the occasion.

Boards that are more active in philanthropy and assist the organization in cultivating donors are characterized as high performing boards. We will be discussing how to improve the board's performance in fundraising and development in a later chapter. Another key characteristic of high performing boards is their ability to evaluate their own performance. I like to say that "Good boards evaluate their chief executive, while great board evaluate themselves." Similar to the process utilized in conducting the organizational assessment, the best way to evaluate your board's performance is to have an outside trained facilitator conduct the assessment. This again involves reviewing important information about the organization and then scheduling confidential interviews. The goal is to measure the level of engagement and motivation of the board to perform at greater levels of success.

In an article that I wrote for The NonProfit Times—*Evaluating the Evaluator: 25 Key Questions for Assessing Your Board Performance,* I wrote that "One of the major overlooked responsibilities of a nonprofit board is the requirement to assess its own performance. I mentioned three possible options: I. I have the board chair and chief executive meet with each member and discuss their thoughts about areas of strength and areas of needed improvement of the board; 2. Utilize a board questionnaire or 3. Have an outside professional facilitator perform the assessment. I strongly advise against option 1. It is not recommended to have your chief executive too involved in assessing the work of the board due to the potential political fallout that might be possible. The vast majority of boards utilize a questionnaire format that calls for a numerical score for each answer. The problem with most, if not all, questionnaires is that they don't allow for open-ended questions and they rarely ask the most important questions getting to the heart of the matter for improving the work of the board:

- Is the board practicing best governance practices?

- Is the board effective in its performance?
- Is the board motivated and engaged? And if not, why not?

My recommendation is to engage an outside trained board facilitator to conduct the assessment through the use of open-ended questions, e.g., do you like being on the board? What is needed to improve the board's work? To dramatically improve the work of the board, one has to assess the level of engagement and motivation of each board member. Only through engaging and motivating your board can nonprofits be in *Strategic Alignment* towards achieving your organization's goals and dreams.

The major obstacles to becoming a high performing board are:

- Failure to fully engage their members
- Failure to actively recruit new members
- Lack of board reappointment criteria
- Inability to select a board chair
- Having an "inner and outer" board (too many executive committee meetings)
- Inability to honestly and constructively address chief executive performance issues
- Poorly run board meetings
- Poor communication to all members
- Nonalignment of organization's vision and goals with committee structures
- Inability to address fears and insecurities of board member related to fundraising and development

High performing boards constantly reexamine themselves and commit themselves to improving their work. Isn't this what the board would expect from their chief executive and his/her staff? It takes courage to take a look inside of oneself. The board needs to demonstrate this courage and move towards being in *Strategic Alignment.*

Let's now turn our attention to Step Six—Impactful Programs and Services: *When to Collaborate, Affiliate or Merge.*

IMPACTFUL PROGRAMS
AND SERVICES

When to Collaborate, Affiliate or Merge.

*"Community cannot for long feed on itself;
it can only flourish with the coming of
others from beyond, their unknown
and undiscovered brothers."*
—Howard Thurman.

Regardless of your mission—education, healthcare, human services, behavioral health, environment, arts & culture, social justice and many important others, programs and services are the core purpose of the nonprofit sector. Your programs and services are the key determinates in generating the level of positive social impact the organization desires. As part of the strategic planning process, these programs and services need to be thoroughly reviewed. To make it easier on the reader, programs and services will hereafter be referred to as programs for the remainder of the chapter.

Questions:
- What programs do we need to improve their performance?
- Which ones do we need to expand?
- What ones do we need to eliminate?

- How responsive are our programs to community needs?
- What innovative programs have we tried to implement?

These are all tough questions that need to be addressed. So where do you start? I recommend that you begin by listing all of your programs on a spread sheet. Next to each program indicate the following:

- Growth or decline of consumer demand for each program for the past three years
- Population estimates for the next five years based on the most recent U. S. Census reports by age groups for each program area, e.g., senior programs would want to know the population estimate of those 65 plus, whereas pre-school programs may want to know the ages of those under the age of 5, etc.
- Percentage of revenue from public and private sources (more on this later in the chapter), e.g. how much is the organization relying upon public funding (local, county, state or federal) compared to private sources of funding
- Information on what tools, if any, your organization utilizes for evaluation and measurement of successful outcomes, results and achievements including, but not limited to, customer satisfaction surveys or focus groups
- Competitor analysis of who else in your area is doing a similar program

In addition to the above, ask yourself this question: How many of your programs are you offering because you applied for and received a grant? How many years is the grant funding promised? If you lose your grant funding, would you continue to offer this program? In my opinion, too many organizations are constantly "chase the money" and then wonder years later why they have negative operating margins. Chasing the money is not an effective strategy for program development. With exceptions of course, I would recommend offering programs that meet the following criteria:

- Demand for the current program is strong and expected to continue
- Population estimates and other demographic data indicate the community need
- Evaluation and measurement tools are developed or in the process of being developed to measure outcomes and results
- Your organization's program has a reputation for excellence
- Private sources of funds are available and expected to continue
- Your organization has a high degree of confidence for embarking on a new program based on reliable community feedback
- The program is not duplicating or competing with the efforts of others who are doing a similar program in the area with a greater record of demonstrated results and outcomes

Financial sustainability is a goal of any strategic planning process, especially in the nonprofit sector.

Review the above recommendations with your senior management team and develop your priority list of program offerings. Identify what improvements, if any, need to be made to enhance or expand the programs. We will discuss how to develop a successful comprehensive funding plan in a later chapter. Next, review those programs that you are constantly losing money on that are draining the financial reserves of your organization. Eliminating programs is one of the toughest decisions any leader needs to make, but it is much better to devote your limited resources to programs that have a higher chance of success than to carry those with very little. This may sound heartless, but you need to look at the bigger picture. Unless you have a credible plan for resource development, you may need to cut your losses. Your organization may not survive when you try to be "all things to all people" and allow one program to make you go under. As a matter of fact, it may give your remaining programs a needed lift of support and spirit.

The higher the percentage of public funding that your organization relies upon for your programs, the greater your risk of being unable to maintain financial sustainability. Everyone knows the financial budgetary deficits at all levels of government—county, state and federal. You need to evaluate during the strategic planning process how you will offer your programs when you are depending far too much on public or government funding. A few of my clients had a 90% or greater percentage of funds from these sources creating tremendous financial uncertainty. A long term goal for every organization is to have a diversified funding base for their programs. The ideal percentage is not to exceed 50-60% of programs relying on public funding. You are at great risk for surviving, let alone succeeding. Don't panic. You won't change overnight, but a key goal of every strategic plan is to take an honest look at how to improve your organization's financial sustainability.

In my first book, "A Guide to Achieving New Heights: The Four Pillars of Successful Nonprofit Leadership," I stated that "Nonprofit was your tax status, not your business plan." As part of your strategic planning process, I implore you to take a fresh look at financially managing your programs in today's challenging environment. We need to remind ourselves of the above quote. I fully understand the importance of mission, but we cannot become blind to the realities of fiscal resources. There is a reason that there is a stereotype of "having a nonprofit mentality." This occurs when the mission and desire to help others is done blindly without considerable thought to your organization's fiscal picture. "It's our mission, we must do this program even if we lose money" is a common response. Though the topic of social entrepreneurism goes well beyond the scope of this book, I strongly encourage my clients to begin to think like social entrepreneurs. Seeking new funding sources is required to maintain and continue your mission.

Today, more than ever before, nonprofit organizations need to develop program evaluation tools and outcome measures. It is no longer acceptable to just provide programs, one needs to determine the results or outcomes of your programs. Today's sophisticated philanthropists want to know their "return on investment." Though we will discuss this more in a later chapter, it is crucial to begin to review the impact and outcome of your programs.

Let's turn to collaboration as a strategic initiative:

Collaboration is a key strategy for program effectiveness and development. You don't need to always go it alone. Corporate and foundation funders also welcome the opportunity to provide funds when a grant application includes a more collaborative approach. Collaboration is a process of working together with another organization to realize shared goals. This process is much deeper than a co-operative venture. It requires a collective determination to reach an identical objective by sharing knowledge and building organizational consensus. Collaboration also requires competent and secure leadership from both sides who can trust and respect each other. Teams that work collaboratively can obtain greater financial resources, recognition and rewards for their efforts, especially when facing competition for finite resources.

The following are a few examples of my clients' recent collaborative efforts.

A prominent Hispanic social agency providing a wide range of support services to the low income and Hispanic community in their area wanted to address the issue of health literacy and education. Statistics clearly indicated that individuals with limited health literacy have less knowledge, worse self-management skills, lower use of preventive services and higher hospitalization rates. Among older adults, inadequate health literacy was independently associated with poorer physical and mental health. Solution: They reached out to a highly regarded teaching medical center in the area to develop a program called *Health Educacion*. Today both organizations are making great strides in improving health literacy, reducing the costs of healthcare costs and improving health outcomes.

As an urban provider of homeless prevention services, many staff members felt they were just "putting a band aid" on the problem. Clients kept returning for the same services each and every month. The facts indicated that over 50% of their clientele had serious mental health issues that were not being addressed. Solution: They contacted a major behavioral healthcare provider in the area who welcomed the chance to develop an outreach program on their site (rent payments helped too). Today, their collaborative effort is finally allowing them to address their clients real underlying issues and "ordering fewer band aids" then ever before. Plus the area political leaders loved the idea of collaboration and are encouraging throughout their large urban city.

A low income provider of pre-school programs in another urban area realized the need for after-care programs for the children and their parents. The vast majority of parents were working full time and needed a secure place for their children until they could be picked up after work. There was little or no funding for such a program. The organization has available space but did not have the resources to develop such a program on their own. The local YMCA was offering after-care programs but their space was limited to accommodate the growing needs in the community. Guess what? Both organizations agreed to collaborate and offer an after-care program at the pre-school program site. Solution: Over 100 new children are now in their collaborative after-school program, the parents are extremely happy and a local corporation likes the idea of collaboration and funded a substantial amount of the program.

A statewide human services organization was in dire need of a comprehensive training program for their professional and administrative staff. The organization has over 500 employees working throughout the state but the need for training on all new technology, corporate compliance and customer service training was not functioning at the level required. Funding was limited to develop and hire their own staff. Solution: They contacted the statewide association for community colleges and arranged to have the continuing education professionals at select college campuses develop a training program for the employees. The employees were better trained at less expense and the community colleges benefited by having increased revenue as well. The Board of Trustees at the human service organization are thrilled at the creative idea of collaboration.

Questions:
- What programs, either existing, expanding, developing or those that may need to close can be enhanced through collaboration?
- Would your board support collaboration?
- Have you asked your funding sources about the idea?

Let's briefly turn to the discussion of mergers in today's nonprofit sector:

When I was a young hospital 37 year old CEO in the 1980's every healthcare consultant was hounding everyone that "If you don't merge now, you will never survive the challenges ahead." Well, that was a scary thought for sure. The reality for the next twenty years is that the overwhelming majority of hospital mergers did not produce the results that were hoped for. Physicians resisted the attempts at implementing clinical best practices, health insurance payers' did not want to offer special rates and administrators refused to give up their organizational control. Today, however, mergers in the healthcare market place are happening at great speed and everyone seems to have learned from past mistakes and mergers are working.

So when is a merger right for you? When does it make strategic sense to explore this option for your organization? Are you asking to discuss a merger or a complete take over?

Mergers and acquisitions can be a very effective strategic goal for your nonprofit organization. However, make sure you know what you are getting involved in and seek outside professional expertise. I've seen too many organizations attempt to merge solely with advice from members of their board. I am sure they are well-meaning but they are exposing your organization and themselves to the potential of significant liability. You will need a professional consultant and a legal advisor who both have extensive experience with mergers and acquisitions in the sector.

When do mergers make sense? When do they not?

Mergers can be very effective when both organizations invest a tremendous amount of time, resources and energy upfront to thoroughly get to know each other. Each organization may bring a wealth of complimentary services, expertise and leadership. They also bring their own baggage and organizational culture (how they go about what they do and how they do it). Mergers can make sense when the combined new organization will offer a wider array of services, improve the efficiency of infrastructure, expanded geographical community outreach, improved fundraising and brand identity. There needs to be a consensus on executive and board leadership for the newly formed merged organization. It often works out very well when one executive director is retiring and another is ready to assume full leadership. There would be far more mergers in the nonprofit sector if there were funds to provide "golden parachutes" to those executives who will not remain after the merger. In the for-profit sector, every executive received compensation and benefits as part of their separation packages.

The following is a recent client example of a successful merger:

Two highly regarded behavioral health organizations began to discuss ways of collaborating on administrative overhead. Do they both need a chief financial officer? Development officer? Marketing and public relations officers? Purchasing director? The two organizations were successful in their respective geographical areas. One was highly regarded for their fee-for-service program while the other was well regarded for their housing programs. The fee-for-service organization wanted to get into housing but had little, if any, experience. The housing specialist did not have success in offering fee-for-service programs and relied heavily on programs that were publicly funded. The two executive directors met often and visited each other's facilities in numerous towns. They served contiguous geographical areas, but did not compete or offer services in each other's respective area. Solution: Both boards met separately at first and then a joint merger steering committee was formed to confidentially explore the possible strategic fit for themselves. After about a year of planning and hard work, a new merged organization was announced to the delight of everyone. The new merged organization became much stronger financially, increased level of executive expertise while providing new services to each respective communities.

The following is an example of what not to do:

Both organizations from the same town were founded over 100 years ago. One was founded to serve immigrants arriving on the shores of America in the early 1900's and one was founded to improve the lives of children and families. One organization was financially sound but wanted to substantially grow its revenue base. The other was in serious financial difficulty, often borrowing money from the board members to make bi-weekly payroll for its employees. Two board members from the struggling organization met with the executive director and board chair from the other organization without inviting their own executive director. The executive director and board chair from the struggling organization even stopped speaking to each other even when in the same room. These secret meetings were held on a regular basis but as would be expected, word leaked out in the community, embarrassing the executive director who was not in the discussions. There was little or no communication to the employees of the organization in trouble and no one to answer their most pressing questions. Will I have a job tomorrow? What does this mean to me? How will this impact those we serve? Well, after months of intensive discussion, the two merged. The struggling organization became a wholly owned subsidiary of the other. Both kept their names. Except the new combined organization decided not to focus their efforts on programs for the growing immigrant population in their town. It was not part of the larger organization's mission. There were many other alternatives for the struggling organization to explore, but panic set in and they basically "sold the organization." Many board members from the minority community were not invited to the new board and the executives from the struggling organization were not offered positions. Many of them should have been dismissed much earlier, but the board from the struggling organization kept "blinders" on to the situation and blamed the executive director solely for the situation they were in. Lesson learned: Invite all stakeholders to the table. Explore all options that might improve both organizations without eliminating key services to certain community groups that might leave them stranded. A merger should improve the strategic position of both organization.

Questions:
- Would your organization benefit from a merger?
- With whom would you want to merge with?
- What would be a successful outcome after the merger?
- Would your community and those you serve be better off if you merged?

Let's now turn to Step Seven—The Positive Brand: What Do People Know Us For.

THE POSITIVE BRAND

What Do People Know Us For

*"Be more concerned with your character
than your reputation, because your character
is what you really are, while your reputation is
merely what others think you are".*
—John Wooden

The concept of developing brand identity is a cornerstone of all for-profit business strategies yet is fairly new for the nonprofit sector. Many nonprofits continue to use their brands primarily as a fundraising tool, but a growing number are moving beyond that approach to explore the wider, strategic roles that brands can play: driving broad, long-term social goals, while strengthening internal identity, cohesion, and capacity. According to a recent study at Harvard University supported by the Rockefeller Foundation, branding is a matter for the entire nonprofit executive team. At every step in an organization's strategy and at each juncture in its theory of change, a strong brand is increasingly seen as critical in helping to build operational capacity, galvanize support, and maintain focus on the social mission.

Brand identity is the total promise that your organization makes to your clients, employees, board, donors and volunteers. Brand identity is the aggregation of all your organization does—its mission, vision, personality and promise to those you serve. It is a means of identifying and distinguishing your organization from others. An organization with a unique brand identity has improved brand awareness, a motivated team of employees who feel proud working for a well branded organization, and active board members and donors. Brand identity leads to brand loyalty, brand preference and high credibility. It assures the customers again and again that you are who you say you are. It establishes an immediate connection between the organization and consumers. Brand identity should be sustainable. It is crucial so that the consumers instantly correlate with your programs and service.

Questions:
- How is your organization different from others?
- What is your "brand" personality?
- Does your organization have brand loyalty and preference?

As part of the *Strategic Alignment* process, your organization should develop the following areas to build a positive identity:

- Review your current core values and make sure that you are actually living them every day. It's one thing to have your values listed on your website and brochure, it is another to make sure they are a reality
- Review your client satisfaction surveys to understand how they feel about your services and

programs and improve your performance where necessary

- Revise and update your website with new content along with video testimonials from those you serve
- Review all of your communication and public relation messages to ensure that they articulate who you are and how you are distinguished from others
- Ensure that all individual and organizational achievements, positive outcomes, results and awards are prominently displayed in your facilities, website and public relations communications
- Discuss your achievements, positive outcomes, results and awards with your employees, board, volunteers, donors and all stakeholders at every opportunity to build strong internal relationships and community ambassadors
- Understand why donors contribute to you and what benefit you have provided them
- Develop a speakers bureau for the community to enable professionals and leadership to present relevant information building strong community relationships

Becoming a "thought leader" in your community is a terrific strategy to help brand your organization. Being a thought leader is becoming a core business strategy for a burgeoning number of professionals, firms and associations. It's difficult to find an exact definition that is universally accepted, but a thought leader is someone who is known for their innovative ideas, expertise, and is widely recognized as a source of guidance in their industry. One of the recurring themes many clients complain about is the lack of community awareness and knowledge of who they are. Too often I hear "We are the best kept secret in town" and I say why is that?

Your organization should organize and coordinate a series of meetings and conferences with community, civic, government, education and business leaders on a range of topics that impact the lives of those in the community. For example, one behavioral health client invited local ministers, police chiefs, court officials, school superintendents, etc., to a series of meetings dealing with "at risk youth." The purpose of these meetings was as follows:

- Demonstrated their expertise on the topic
- Provided an opportunity to build a reputation as a leading community advocate
- Build new relationships with key leaders in the community
- Enhance ability to receive grant funding through collaboration
- Coordinate a regional community plan of action
- Generate positive public relations and visibility

Additional topics related to senior and disabled independent living, housing, healthcare reform and other emerging community issues were addressed in future meetings.

Identifying trends at an early stage or creating ideas that change the future for the community are characteristics of being a thought leader. Another of the positive results of being a thought leader is to increase your organization's name recognition in the community. By outreach to the community, new programs or enhanced existing programs could be developed based on emerging community need and funding identified by those willing to invest in successful patient outcomes.

Every successful nonprofit organization is a brand. When we think of the American Red Cross, Make-A-Wish Foundation of America or the Bill & Melinda Gates Foundation, what comes to your mind is a very well branded nonprofit organization. These are iconic nonprofits whose very name conjures up a host of associations, memories and positive feelings. Branding is not just marketing and advertising (though they are key activities promoting your brand). Larry Checco, nonprofit consultant and author of *Branding for Success: A Roadmap for Raising the Visibility and Value of Your Nonprofit Organization*, says that every organization can use branding to create visibility and convince supporters of your organization's value.

Questions:
- What is your organization's brand?
- What is your branding strategy?
- What is the message you want people to hear?
- What do you want people to really know about who you are?

One suggestion for you to consider is to develop a few focus groups for your organization from people in your community. Keep the group's small (more than eight but less than twenty) to better manage the discussion. Ask them open ended questions about the following:

- When you hear our name, what feelings and thoughts come to mind?
- What is our reputation in the community?
- Do we properly communicate our values?
- Do we demonstrate our commitment to client service?
- What does our brand represent?

With all the focus today on social media and mobile technology, we often forget how important your website plays a role in branding your organization. You don't need to spend a fortune to have a decent website but it should be kept up-to-date. If your Home page is still showing a picture of your gala from three years ago, it's a good time to make changes. According to FlashMint blog, an online website developer, your website should have the following key features:

- An eye-catching design. What is attracting visitors first is your design, it should not be dull or too flashy
- Convenient navigation. Visitors coming to your website should be able to easily "surf" through and interface with other links
- Proper content. What users want is up-to-date information. Once disappointed, they rarely come back looking for more information
- Contact information. Make sure all users can easily contact you via phone or email
- Search option. Provide all visitors with the help of a search field so they can easily obtain information

- Sign-up form. It is very important for users not to spend hours in search of "Sign-Up" or "Register Here" buttons
- Sitemap. Make sure a list of links leading to all pages in your website is clearly visible
- Web Browsers Compatibility. Make sure your site is compatible with the many web browsers available
- Images. Make sure all of the pictures and photos are in the proper format, neither too large or too pixelated
- Analytics. Statistics and analytics help you discover how people find your website, who links to you and how many hits you have and so on

A monthly or quarterly newsletter highlighting any recent achievement or success is another key component of your branding strategy. It should keep your stakeholders updated with possible links back to your website. I highly recommend to many organizations who are just starting a newsletter to consider utilizing Constant Contact, an inexpensive online tool for creating newsletters, social media marketing and online surveys. Constant Contact, Inc. wrote the book on Engagement Marketing™—the new marketing success formula that helps small organizations create and grow customer relationships in today's socially connected world. Through its unique combination of online marketing tools and free personalized coaching, Constant Contact helps small businesses, associations, and nonprofits connect and engage with their next great customer, client, or member. Launched in 1998, Constant Contact has long championed the needs of small organizations, providing them with an easy and affordable way to create and build successful, lasting customer relationships.

Another key recommendation for creating your brand on your website is through the use of a web-based video. The best people to tell your story are often the ones who receive services from you. It is relatively easy to produce a 3-5 minute video for your website that will appeal to both their minds and hearts. This video may begin with the Executive Director or Board Chair providing a warm welcome to be followed by testimonials and photos of those served by your organization. You may also want to have a key donor or two included in the video to explain why they support your organization. It is amazing what powerful, heartfelt stories your clients can tell.

One final thought on branding. I think it is very effective for nonprofit organizations to let people know who serves on your board, their professional background and expertise. Of course, no personal information or contact information should be displayed but I think your board reflects who you are and I think they should be prominently displayed under About Us. I also think the leadership team with photos and titles and contact information should be readily available.

Let's now turn to Step Eight—Seeking Investors, Not Just Funders: Why Giving to Success Makes $ense.

SEEKING INVESTORS,
NOT JUST FUNDERS

Seeking Investors Not Just Funders:
Why Giving to Success Makes $ense

"It's not how much we give but
how much love we put into giving."
—Mother Teresa

Now you need to develop a comprehensive fundraising plan to secure the financial resources to support the programs and services in your plan. Every nonprofit organization relies upon the philanthropic support of others. Yet, despite all of the knowledge about fundraising, most nonprofit organizations struggle in this area. This chapter will address the many challenges that most organizations face and provide a new fresh approach to engage your board and chief executive to move your organization forward.

Let me know if the following statement describes your organization—*Board members would rather "stick pins" in their eyes than have anything to do with raising money.* The mere mention of the word "fundraising" creates anxiety and discomfort. Why is this? There are a number of reasons, but the biggest is the fear of rejection. Another reason is "If I ask them for money, they may ask me for money." Is this true for your board?

Another problem for many organizations is that they view the Development Office as a department—like finance, human resources or quality improvement. The development efforts are disconnected from the work of the organization. Boards do not see the connection between the organization's success and the success of their fundraising efforts. Development needs to be an attitude integrated into all aspects of the organization not just a department down the hall. I will shortly describe what I call the "fundraising Bermuda triangle and how to avoid it. And too many organizations ask for money because of their financial distress than their organizational success—a term I coined "The tin cup theory of fundraising."

How many of you have experienced the following:

Your board development committee meets and the chairperson calls the meeting to order. They review the fundraising plan for the upcoming year—*There is talk about the gala—Who can we honor and where should it be held? Where is this year's golf outing and who will agree to chair it? How about the wine tasting—how much can we raise? The committee reviews the standard list of donor prospects that were assigned to each committee member and the chair says "Did anyone call their list of prospects? A long silence and then "OK, let's move on to discuss the table settings for the gala. Let's put this on next month's agenda, hopefully more people will attend the meeting. Leaving little accomplished and little achieved.*

The overwhelming number of people who serve on your boards are well meaning people, they want to do the right thing—they want your organization to succeed—but why doesn't it happen—why does everything that deals with fundraising feel like pulling teeth? Let's start our discussion with an understanding of why people really give money—the Principles of Philanthropy.

- They give because they want to
- They give because they have been asked
- They give to people they respect and trust
- They give to success—not distress
- They give to meet the needs of those you serve— not to your needs
- They give to make the world a better place

Most people's concept of fundraising is the "tin cup theory." When I was a boy growing up in New Jersey, I can remember my mom taking me and my brothers and sister to the Radio City Music Hall Christmas Show with the famous Rockettes. We always took a bus into New York City and arrived at the Port Authority bus terminal. There was always remember an older man with one leg holding up a tin cup with pencils in front of the terminal begging for money. Thus my early perception of fundraising was begging for your needs, hence the "tin cup theory." Many nonprofit organizations today still practice and promote the concept of asking for money based on your needs. Your organizational needs for new facilities, program support, etc., are important, but that is not an effective way to go about it. Your fundraising efforts will become more successful when you begin to frame your fundraising discussions on investing in your success.

Based on the researched principles of philanthropy, people give to success, not to distress. Those organizations that have transitioned from the "tin cup" to the "investment theory" have far more success in raising money. Their board members are more comfortable and less fearful of rejection when they ask people to invest in your success, in your positive achievements and results, to documented outcomes and how you make a difference in the lives of others. Their board members are more externally focused on what they do for others and not on what the needs of the organization are. Those organizations that develop a culture of philanthropy where everyone understands the principles of philanthropy dramatically increase their level of success in today's fierce competition for the donor dollar.

Questions:
- What are your organization's most recent achievements?
- What success do you have for donors to invest in?
- How do you communicate your success to your stakeholders?

In all of the thousands of book on fundraising and development, there is one concept that I have rarely heard mentioned is that the key to further engage and motivate your board, is the need to increase your board's level of self-confidence. We have huge unrealistic expectations of our board members related to fundraising. Just because someone is president of the regional bank or vice president of business development for a successful area corporation does not guarantee or translate to success in the world of fundraising and development. In addition, constantly reminding board members about their role and responsibility as a board member on fundraising is like reminding your kids to clean their room. It rarely is effective (maybe your kids but not mine). When people become confident in their abilities, they generate their own motivation.

Also, during the board recruitment process, the issue of fundraising is rarely brought up by many nonprofit organizations. Yet we expect our boards to know about fundraising and become disappointed when their performance is less than expected. We need to continually educate our board members on why people give money. The more comfortable and knowledgeable your board becomes, the more their level of engagement and activities will increase. In addition to the personal satisfaction and joy that comes from giving, one of the major reasons why people give money, based on the principles of philanthropy, is because they were asked by someone they know and respect. It is often as simple as that.

Let's now discuss how to avoid the "fundraising Bermuda triangle."

The fundraising Bermuda triangle is when all three parties, development officer, chief executive and board, all point fingers and blame each other for their organization's lack of success. This is based on a lack of solid knowledge and understanding that each role plays (the triangle) in moving the fundraising initiatives forward. Apparently it is easier to blame others than to own up to their own personal responsibility. It takes a team effort of all three parties,

The average tenure of a development officer is about 18 months. The constant turnover is usually due to the lack of any significant support from either the chief executive officer and/or members of the board. Far too often, board members ask the chief executive "How much money did she raise yet? Heck, she's already been on the payroll for over three months!" Common complaints from the development officer are "My CEO won't help me out" or "my board expects me to do it all by myself, they won't make any introductions to their friends for me." Board members often refuse to feel any responsibility for fundraising when they make statements like "I'll join your board as long as I don't have to raise any money" and they hear "sure, no problem, we don't expect you to, we have our own development department."

When everyone understands the basic principles of philanthropy and the role each is expected to perform, the "Bermuda triangle" can be avoided. Let's review the role of each now:

The Role of the Chief Executive

- Chief sales officer—let people know what you do
- Chief relationship officer—be the face of the organization
- Chief communications officer—let people know your achievements and success
- Chief brand builder—build positive images of your organization
- Chief fundraising officer—be responsible for increasing donors and dollars

The Role of the Board

- Advocate for your mission
- Communicate your achievements and outcomes
- Identify and cultivate prospective donors
- Active participator in special events
- Write personal notes and letters on annual appeals

- Make annual personal contribution
- Ask someone for a gift or become a co-solicitor
- Recognize and thank donors

The Role of the Development Officer

- Develop comprehensive and diversified fundraising plan
- Create written case for support
- Quarterback the game
- Build prospect relations
- Follow through on all initiatives
- Develop and maintain donor data base
- Educate the CEO and board
- Solicit gifts
- Provide effective stewardship

When everyone learns that development is a team effort, not a solo practice, the organization will avoid the Bermuda triangle and achieve greater levels of success. Each party understands their own role and what is expected of them and what they can expect of others. When the organization avoids the Bermuda triangle, they are becoming an organization that is in *Strategic Alignment*.

Since we now know that people give to success not distress, make sure every board member, chief executive and development officer can answer these:

Questions:
- What is the value we provide to our community?
- What are our top achievements and results from this past year?

- What is the return on investments that our donors provide us?
- Why are we worthy of someone's gift?

As far as the mechanics and specifics of building a comprehensive fundraising plan, I highly recommend reading *Achieving Excellence in Fund Raising* by Hank Rosso. I have found it to be the most comprehensive book providing in-depth discussion on how to build a comprehensive fundraising plan. The book effectively describes that effective fundraising is dependent on an effective planning and rigorous execution—actually more planning than execution. The better the planning, the better the fundraising results. Rosso's fundraising cycle illustrates the principal that it is possible to ask someone for a gift too soon. A premature gift solicitation usually leads to one of two outcomes: the donor refuses to make a gift (because they have not been properly cultivated and connected to your organization), or they give a token gift that is neither appropriate based on their gift capacity nor adequate for your organization's need. Neither outcome is what you would want. Again, read and learn Rosso's fundraising cycle to avoid these outcomes and pave the way to the preferred response "Yes, I'll make the gift you asked for." To paraphrase a winemaker's advertising slogan, "We will solicit no gift before it's time."

Jerold Panas is the successful author of a number of bestselling books on fundraising. Two of his most popular books are *Asking: A 59 Minute Guide to Everything Board Members, Volunteers and Staff Must Know to Secure the Gift* and *The Fundraising Habits of Supremely Successful Boards: A One Hour Guide to Ensuring Your Organization's Future.* These books are an excellent resource guide for your board members, especially those new to fundraising. I would like to mention some of the key characteristics of successful fundraising organizations according to Panas:

- Integrity rules
- Mission is everything
- Never lose sight that they change lives
- Continually push for success
- Willing to leave comfort zone
- They have an inspiring vision and a plan to achieve it
- Extremely passionate about who they are
- Maintain positive attitude
- Engaged and inspired leadership
- 100% of Board members contribute annually
- Constantly seeking fresh new faces for the board
- Always acknowledging and thanking donors

When your board begins to connect integrity, passion and the "investment theory of fundraising" with the integration of effective board governance, inspiring leadership and visionary thinking your organization will dramatically increase donors and dollars and be in *Strategic Alignment*.

Let's now turn to Step Nine—Successfully Executing The Plan: How to Build The Bicycle While Riding It.

SUCCESSFULLY
EXECUTING THE PLAN

Learn How to Build The Bicycle While Riding It

*"The execution of the laws is
more important than the making them."*
—*Thomas Jefferson*

I hope you have enjoyed reading this book and the key strategic steps described within on how to build an effective, results oriented strategic plan. I also hope that the book has inspired you to develop the necessary leadership competencies to ensure your organization successfully achieves its vision and goals. Now that we have developed the strategic plan, however, the key to achieving your dreams is successful execution.

Strategic planning gets all the cachet, but the most creative, visionary strategic plan is useless unless is fully executed and becomes reality. Based on numerous research studies, however, execution is a major challenge for most corporations, let alone nonprofit organizations. Estimates indicate that nearly 60% of organizations have difficulty executing the strategies that were formulated during the planning stage. The reasons for poor execution are many, but some of the major reasons are:

- Poor implementation training of those responsible for execution
- Resistance to managing change
- Self-interest versus organizational interest
- Maintaining existing functioning silos and political in-fighting
- The lack of clear communication and not fully monitoring progress.
- Disconnect between planning objectives and operational realities

The key requirements for successful execution are:

- Having the right leadership in place to drive and lead the execution
- Clearly communicated objectives, tasks and goals
- A means of keeping track of your progress towards achieving your goals; and
- Clear responsibility and accountability
- Rewards and recognition for those employees and/or departments that have executed the strategies in the plan

Based on my experience, too many people wait for the strategic plan to be completed before beginning to make any changes. One of my favorite saying is "Sometimes you have to build a bicycle while riding it." This means quite simply, you cannot afford to wait for the plan to be completed before you begin to implement the strategies contained in the plan. The following are some of my basic recommendations:

- In order to build momentum, address the "low hanging fruit" first. These may include changes to your website, logo or inclusion of the names of your board on the website. Don't tackle the most difficult changes first, gaining success early on leads to positive morale and confidence building.
- Identify those changes that are the most politically difficult and develop a long-term strategy for addressing those.
- Consistently communicate to your board and management team all changes, regardless of how minor they may seem. Create a report that indicates those items where the strategy has been achieved by a green light, yellow or caution light where actions are in progress and red light, where no action or results has been achieved.

Consider transitioning your organization from a culture of planning to one of managing for results and outcomes. Too often, strategic planning is detached from day-to-day operations. It may be valuable to your organization to spend more management time on reporting achievements than on reporting problems. I remember early on in my career as a hospital CEO, I asked for written reports from the management team on what their achievements were for the month. Their response was "We never did this before" and I said "Exactly, this is what I want you to focus on, achievements not problems." It is amazing what people can accomplish when they begin to get rewarded and recognized for their success.

I strongly believe that every individual has the potential to develop into a truly effective leader and that every organization has the ability to achieve their dreams. I have seen firsthand organizations that had poor images, poor morale, and poor financial performance develop into tremendous community assets by following and implementing the strategic steps outlined in this book:

- The Assessment—How to Discover Your Organization's Soul
- The Vision—What Are Your Dreams
- The Process—How to Build Your Plan
- Executive Leadership: Why Today's CEO Means Chief Entrepreneurial Officer
- High Performing Boards—How to Fully Engage Your Board
- Impactful Programs and Services—When to Collaborate, Affiliate or Merge
- The Positive Brand—What Do People Know Us For
- Seeking Investors, Not Just Funders—Why Giving to Success Makes $ense
- Successfully Executing The Plan—How to Build the Bicycle While Riding It

The fun in life is accepting challenges with a positive attitude and in developing those around us to work together towards a common vision. There will be many day-to-day challenges that you must confront, and at times it may be difficult to see the light at the end of the tunnel. However, you must work through this difficult period. Everyone that I know who has achieved a level of success, worked very hard to get there.

At your organization becomes in *Strategic Alignment*, you will experience the excitement of having accomplished something very special. You will see the dramatic results of your hard work. Success does not happen overnight. There may be times when you feel your efforts are fruitless, when you wonder if in fact, you can move your organization forward. There may be times when financial concerns seem overpowering, when staff morale is low, or when board members and key leadership resign. Many people in your organization are comfortable with the way things are. You will be challenged on why you are moving the organization forward towards a new vision. Don't let any of these things discourage you.

There were many difficult days for me when I became the chief executive officer of both hospitals I led. I had to establish my credibility, build relationships and communicate my vision and my plan to achieve it. Just like a football coach before a big game, I had to give passionate speeches about how we were going to be victorious. One of the key responsibilities of an effective leader is getting your team members to believe in themselves. Whatever, your organization's current circumstance, remember the passion you have for your mission and the vision you have for your organization.

Truly effective leaders create a vision for their organization. It takes courage to lead, particularly when you are caught up in managing so many day-to-day challenges. Still, a passionate and inspiring leader is responsible for creating the vision and building a plan to make that vision become a reality. Overcoming obstacles and challenges creates real leaders. Think positive and develop a can-do attitude. By following the key strategic steps necessary to go beyond the traditional strategic planning process, your organization will achieve long term success and sustainability.

The process of aligning all stakeholders, both internally and externally, to be focused and committed to achieving one goal: the organization's vision is a must. This innovative concept requires the development of new leadership competencies and non-traditional skills for both today's nonprofit executives and board leadership. I wish you much success and good will on your new journey to move your organization into *Strategic Alignment*.

BIBLIOGRAPHY

Burt Anus, *Visionary Leadership: Creating a Compelling Sense of Direction for Your Organization,* Wiley & Sons, 1995

Bryan W. Barry, *Strategic Planning Workbook for Nonprofit Organizations,* Amherst H. Wilder Foundation, 1997

Richard P. Chait, William P. Ryan, and Barbara E. Taylor, *Governance as Leadership: Reframing the Work of Nonprofit Boards.* John Wiley & Sons, 1992

Michael A. Sand, *How to Manage an Effective Nonprofit Organization,* Career Press, Incorporated, 2005

John Carver, *BOARDS That Make a Difference: A New Design for Leadership in Nonprofit and Public Organizations,* Wiley & Sons, 2011

John Carver and Miriam Carver, *A Carver Policy Governance Guide, Evaluating the CEO and Board Performance,* Wiley & Sons, 2009

Deborah L. Kocsis and Susan A. Waechter, *Driving Strategic Planning: A Nonprofit Executive's Guide,* BoardSource, 2003

Mark Light, *The Strategic Board: The Step-By-Step Guide to High-Impact Governance,* Wiley & Sons, 2001

Dennis C. Miller, *A Guide to Achieving New Heights: The Four Pillars of Successful Nonprofit Leadership,* AuthorHouse, 2007

Dennis C. Miller, The Nonprofit Board Therapist: A Guide to Unlocking Your Organization's True Potential, AuthorHouse, 2010

Sally J. Patterson, Generating Buzz: Strategic Communications for Nonprofit Boards, BoardSource, 2006

Eugene Temple, *Achieving Excellence in Fundraising,* Jossey—Bass, 2003

Cathy A. Trower, *The Practitioner's Guide to Governance as Leadership: Building High Performing Nonprofit Boards*

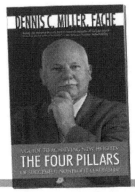

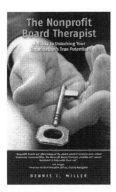

"*Though I have observed the success of many organizations, far too many never achieve the level of success they desire because they fail to understand the importance of integrating board governance, leadership, visioning and philanthropy. My goal is to provide a roadmap on how to unlock the true potential of your nonprofit organization. I hope this book will inspire and motivate you to find the courage and develop the confidence to pursue your organization's dreams and goals.*"

Dennis C. miller
Author, *The Nonprofit Board Therapist*

Book Testimonials:

"*The Non-Profit Therapist is a must read for any non-profit board member or CEO. Dennis' book contains numerous nuggets of wisdom that would assist any non-profit organization. The suggestions are practical and easy to implement. If your organization is experiencing issues around good governance and leadership, make the time to read this book.*"

David Williams, President & Chief Executive Officer
Make-A-Wish Foundation of America

"*The Nonprofit Board Therapist offers much wise advice that we can all benefit.*"

Risa Lavisso-Mourey, M.D., M.B.A., President and CEO
Robert Wood Johnson Foundation

"*A good educational tool should embody new perspectives, be evidence-based and stand the test of best practice. Dennis Miller's new book on unlocking the true potential of nonprofit boards embodies all three of these values to learn the right to be rated as a good educational tool!*"

Thomas Harvey, Director of Nonprofit Professional Development
Mendoza College of Business, University of Notre Dame

Made in the USA
San Bernardino, CA
12 December 2015